Victi

ED
by l

MARCEL CALLO
by M. N. L. Couve de Murville

TITUS BRANDSMA
by Hugh Clarke

*All booklets are published thanks to the
generous support of the members of the
Catholic Truth Society*

CATHOLIC TRUTH SOCIETY
PUBLISHERS TO THE HOLY SEE

CONTENTS

Preface

"At the end of the second millennium the Church has once again become a Church of martyrs" (*Tertio Millennio Adveniente*); so wrote the Pope in preparation for the year 2000. It is a reminder that the celebration of an anniversary, of the passage of time as such, is not enough. Time must be redeemed by Christ. An anniversary recalls crimes as well as acts of heroism. This is certainly true of our twentieth century which has seen the carnage of two world wars and the unspeakable horrors of the concentration camps.

The redemptive work of Christ is manifested in the lives of men and women who are his followers. The Church has always been careful to preserve the records of those who were outstanding in the service of God and their fellow human beings. As the Pope says, "the *martyrologium* of the first centuries was the basis of the veneration of the Saints. By proclaiming and venerating the holiness of her sons and daughters, the Church gave the supreme honour to God himself; in the martyrs she venerated Christ, who was the origin of their martyrdom and their holiness." (*Tertio Millennio Adveniente*.)

That is why the CTS is republishing the lives of seven victims of the Nazi regime in Germany. As recorded in the two booklets *Victims of the Nazis*, these are the stories of one German Jewess, two German priests, two laymen (one Austrian the other French) and two friars (one a Pole and the other a Dutchman). They all chose to lay down their lives rather than accept an evil political system based on totalitarianism and racism. They died because of their fidelity to Christ and his Church. Their witness must not be forgotten.

M. N. L. Couve de Murville
St Chad's, Birmingham, June 1997

EDITH STEIN

by
Monk Matthew

Edith Stein was a German Jewess who descended to the intellectual heights of atheism, was converted to Roman Catholicism and as a Discalced Carmelite nun ascended to Mount Carmel to the crystal peaks of mysticism. Her life on earth ended in the gas chambers of a Nazi concentration camp – which she entered unresisting as an oblation for her race.

Spiritually a giant, in body she was small and frail and insignificant: at first meeting she often disappointed those who had known her only by her fame as a major contemporary philosopher.

She will also be known as a very great Discalced Carmelite, but most of all, perhaps, she will be known as a Saint for converts.

Early Life

Edith Stein was born on the Feast of St Wilfred, 12th October 1891, in the then German town of Breslau (now Wroclaw in Poland). She was the youngest of seven children whose natural gaiety was moderated by an aura of culture, learning, and the strict respectability which Germany shared with Victorian England.

The Stein family was wealthy, and middle-class. Herr Stein had a timber business. In their large, richly furnished home, under the dominant influence of a devout mother, every appropriate ceremonial of the Talmud (the Rabbinic laws and teachings) was precisely observed: grace was said in Hebrew, prayers were regularly offered and religious customs were precisely carried out.

A deeply religious, happy, prosperous, respected and cultured German family, it exhibited the Jewish regard for learning and 'position'. Suddenly, Edith's father died. She was three years old, too young perhaps to know the depths of tragedy and no doubt sheltered from grief by brothers, sisters, relations.

Dependency on God, and only God, which is the 'all' of Discalced Carmelite spirituality may have been planted at this time. Even a three year old can experience sub-conscious shock. Her mother, who had been all things at all times to the little child, now, suddenly and without the explanations such a little one could comprehend, had to break off much of their earlier indulgent relationship.

Suddenly, it was the elder sister to whom Edith had to turn for her needs and wants. Suddenly, it was aunties and cousins who were dressing her neatly and taking her for the daily afternoon walks and picnics and visits to the town's crumbling ramparts and beautiful gardens, or to hear the band playing in the park. Her mother, she was not to know, was immersing herself in learning and running the timber business – which was to prosper mightily under her busy and efficient drive.

At first Edith seems to have filled some of the gap by playing more with other children, but she was a small, pale and delicate child towards whom more robust playmates behaved condescendingly. So she turned increasingly to her sisters. They were diligent students, much given to home studies and learning, and taking her own part in this sort of activity quickly became the child's major conscious motivation and ambition.

She also had her mother's drive and clever mind. When she was no more than four years old, Edith was giving vent to such thoughts as: 'Whoever lies once is never believed, even when he speaks the truth!'

In the years that followed, her god was intellectual achievement. It was that which had her respect; it was on that her drive, effort and ambition focused; it was in that she sought praise and recognition. From the age of four she spent the whole of her school life at the best and most modern school – Victoria School on the outskirts of Breslau;

from the outset she was recognised as being unusually advanced for her age. Hard-working as well as gifted, and possessed of an iron will, she went on shining throughout her school years. In the senior college, where exceptionally stiff entrance examinations meant that all the pupils were extremely gifted, Edith Stein 'was some way above all others in ability and knowledge'.

This is not to say that she was a hard, thrusting little go-getter. On the contrary, biographies show in these early years a warm and loving nature, always patient, kind and helpful, taking part in the school's social amusements and having that sympathetic aura which meant that, as one contemporary put it: 'You could tell her all your troubles and secrets, and she was always earnest with advice and gentle with help, and any confidence was safe with her'. She had, in short, that rare combination – intellectual brilliance and a warm gift for friendship.

Atheism and Philosophy

Spiritually, however, she was causing her mother concern. Frau Stein confided to friends: 'Edith is clever but not pious, with no religious convictions and showing little interest in Judaism.' True, when at home on vacation, she went to the synagogue and joined in the scrupulously observed rituals of the home out of a deep devotion to her mother, but we know from Edith Stein herself that at this period she considered herself an atheist.

She looked from afar and with awe on the famed intellects of the time, including Dr Karl Stern, professor of philosophy at Breslau University, Edmund Husserl, inventor of a whole new branch of philosophy and Max Scheler, famous throughout Europe for the power and brilliance of his lectures.

But the spiritual inner life which Christ was later to 'bring to perfection' can be seen in retrospect to have been nourished through childhood by her unconscious absorption of the values of the deeply religious home, infused and nurtured by the devout example, prayer and petitions of her mother.

From the Breslau Girls' College, young Edith passed to Breslau University. She entered the Philosophy School, where one of her idols, Karl Stern, was Professor.

He and Edith were immediately attracted to each other, and it is significant that although neither of them knew it at the time, Stern, another Jew, was also travelling Edith's road. Some years later he, too, was to become a Roman Catholic. If it were an isolated incident it may not be very convincing as evidence of the 'hand of God' in Edith Stein's spiritual development, but there are many other examples of the workings of Providence in her life.

After two years Edith transferred to what, in those 'atheist' days was regarded as the temple of free thought – the famous Gottingen University, where, it was said, 'philoso-

phy is talked day and night, at table, and on the street –
everywhere.' Before long she was a personal friend of, and
was being treated as an equal by, the Professor whom she
had for long regarded as the 'philosopher of our day' –
Edmund Husserl.

Approaching conversion

Hiking with friends one day through the mountains, dusk
found them near a farmhouse, where they lodged overnight.
In the morning the owner and his workmen, as was their
habit, gathered in prayer before setting off to their tasks.
She was later to say this first glimpse of the Roman
Catholic faith made 'a deep impression' on her. Soon after
this, Max Scheler gave a series of lectures to the
Philosophical Society which Edith attended. Max was a
Roman Catholic first and a philosophy lecturer second, and
his philosophy lectures were so well developed that, as
Edith wrote; 'He propagated Catholic ideas with all the brilliance of his intellect and power of expression. This was
contact with a world which had so far remained unknown to
me.' She was not yet ready for the faith, but 'it opened up
for me a whole region of phenomena which I could no
longer ignore.'

Her conversion was being moulded in the inner depths of
the soul, but at the outer level of the intellect she did not
immediately make time to look further into the claims
which God, through Max Scheler, had set in motion. What

happened, she says, is that it brought doubts to her atheism, and 'eventually put rationalist prejudice to flight.'

One of Edith's professors was a certain Adolph Reinach. In 1914 he volunteered for the War and went to the trenches. Edith, quite independently, dropped her studies and joined the Red Cross, where the 'compassion, patience and warm helpfulness' which had marked her earlier years became further developed through caring for the sick and wounded in a hospital for patients with contagious diseases. She did this for two years.

Professor Reinach and his young wife were both Catholic converts. When he was killed on the Western front in 1917 his young widow requested Edith to come and arrange her late husband's philosophy papers. Edith readily went to the house expecting, with her inbred Jewish attitude to death, to find a woman broken and desolate with sorrow. Instead, she found this young convert from Judaism calm and quietly joyful in the strength and inner peace of Christ's revelations and promises.

We can see God's influence in this, and so in time could Edith, for, years later, she wrote: 'It was then that I first encountered the Cross and the divine strength which it inspires in those who bear it. For the first time I saw before my eyes the Church, born of Christ's redemptive suffering, victorious over the sting of death. It was the moment in which my unbelief was shattered, Judaism paled, and Christ streamed out upon me – Christ in the mystery of the Cross.'

That, however, was written from the rarefied mystical heights she went on to ascend. At the time, she remained unaware. She had in 1916 accepted the position of assistant to the Professor under whom she had earlier taken her Doctorate of Philosophy – the renowned Husserl, now Professor of Philosophy at the University of Freiburg.

She caused a sensation in the world of philosophers with a brilliant essay on 'Plant-soul – Animal-soul – Human-soul', which shocked her atheist friends because 'it showed that she was no longer a Rationalist: it revealed a revival of faith in God.'

Deeper stirrings

Of this period she was later to write: 'My soul, yet unrecognised, was as earth without water, thirsting for the living waters of Truth. I had not then begun to pray, but this longing for Truth was a prayer in itself.'

But the inner preparation was nearing fulfilment; her conversion was now imminent. Like St Augustine with his famous enlightenment in a garden, many converts see in retrospect some particular incident or experience which marks their conversion, and Edith Stein is no exception. At Freiburg she was often invited by colleague Dr Conrad-Martius and husband to spend weekends on their fruit farm at Bergzabern, where Edith enjoyed fruit-picking and generally mucking-in with the family. The Conrad-Martius family, although Protestants, appear to have had a good number of Roman Catholic books in their bookcases.

One can almost see God influencing these people to buy 'The Life of St Teresa of Avila Written by Herself', influencing the friendship between them and Edith, influencing them to be called urgently away during this weekend Edith was staying with them, and influencing Mrs Martius to hurry away with the parting invitation to Edith, left alone in the farmhouse, to help herself to any book she wanted from the bookcase.

Edith tells us: 'I picked at random and took out a large volume. I began to read it, was at once captivated, and did not stop until I reached the end. As I closed the book I said: "That is the Truth."' It was St Teresa's 'Life'.

A remarkable thing happened that weekend, when you consider that, at the conscious level, Edith was by now a former atheist groping around in the uncertain world of agnosticism. Consider the spirituality of St Teresa. It is of the highest order of mysticism. It is the language of the soul, and it communicates itself only to those in whom spirituality is alive – even if, as in Edith's case at the time, that inner life is unrecognised by the conscious mind.

This says much about the inner preparation which had been going on within, for the incident of Edith's 'weekend with St Teresa' – as with St Augustine's 'garden' and the incidents which mark 'the moment of conversion' for many, many converts – was the moment of emergence of a

God-awareness which had been alive and building up towards fruition beneath an enclosing outer crust for many years.

We can see, too, that God now brought into play the other qualities he had allowed to develop within her. Her perfectionism, her singularity of purpose, would henceforth centre on Christ. She had found the 'treasure hidden in a field' (*Mt* 13:44) and all else would shrink to relative unimportance. She had found the true and eternal object of her abundance of love, and the world-centred values of her intellectual atheism were revealed in all their dark emptiness; things that had been of supreme value were of no value, and that which had been of no value would now assume supreme value.

Baptism

From that weekend onwards Edith Stein became the complete convert, living for Christ alone, and her singularity and extremism – a characteristic of all the saints – at once made her want to reject the world totally. She wanted to enter a Discalced Carmelite convent without delay, and give herself wholly to the solitary contemplative 'Way' mapped by St Teresa and St John of the Cross, travelling alone through prayer and contemplation towards the mystical condition.

It was late into the night at the fruit farm when she finished absorbing the impact of her 'experience', and first thing next morning she went into the town and bought a Roman Catholic Catechism and a Missal. Her fine mind quickly mastered their meaning and there is something delightfully innocent in the way she set off, as soon as she had finished reading, to the Roman Catholic church in Bergzabern to ask for Baptism!

When she got to the church Mass was about to begin, and the reality of the preparation that had been going on within is again evidenced in her comment: 'It was the first time I had ever been in a Catholic church, but nothing was strange to me... I understood even the smallest ceremonies.'

After Mass she followed the priest – 'a saintly-looking old man' she calls him – into the presbytery and astonished him by, quite simply, asking for Baptism there and then. He protested that it was necessary to be instructed and greatly prepared before being received into the Church. 'How long have you been receiving instruction and who has been giving it?' The only answer Edith could think of was: 'Please, your reverence, test my knowledge.'

A theological discussion followed, with the priest becoming progressively more amazed not just by this frail Jewess's knowledge of the doctrines of the Catholic Church which she had absorbed from the Catechism and Missal she had brought, but by her understanding and 'feeling' for Christ. The discussion ended in a firm arrangement that

Edith Stein would be received into the Church on 1st January, 1922.

She spent the entire preceding night in prayers of preparation, and early in the morning our Lord received her through the Sacraments of Baptism and Holy Communion. For her Baptismal name she chose – Teresa.

The brilliant intellectual and learned philosopher was now an obedient child of the Church. She went now to do what she was to describe as the most painful thing she had to face during her entire life on earth–to confront her mother, whom she loved deeply, with the news that she had been converted to Christ. Her mother wept. It was the first time her children had ever seen their mother weep. Edith wept with her. She stayed at home for six months, of which time her mother was to tell an intimate friend: 'I have never seen anyone pray like Edith'. She was praying, she tells us, that the unity of this loving Stein family would not be broken.

Teaching at a Convent School

Then, on Candlemas Day 1922, Edith Stein was confirmed in the Cathedral at Speyer, where God had ready and waiting for her the spiritual director for the next phase of her progress, one Canon Schwind.

Taking the name 'Teresa' in Baptism was more than admiration or gratitude to the great foundress of the Order of Discalced Carmelites whose influence had opened Edith's spiritual eyes. Rather, it was an immediate affinity with the Saint's spirituality – and Edith yearned only to enter Carmel.

Part of her testing must surely have been the anguish of our Lord's apparent rebuff to this plan, for Canon Schwind would not hear of it, but advised her, instead, to apply for the position of principal teacher in the Dominican Convent School at Speyer, which had fallen vacant.

Thus, in the world's eyes, she plunged from the high office of Professor of Philosophy at a renowned university to a relatively lowly task at a girls' training college for teachers. She accepted this as God's will for her, and we can see how God was, in fact, answering her prayer. At the convent school, it was arranged that she would have her own room. Here she studied, wrote and prayed. She had the Chapel for daily Mass and for the hours she spent in prayer to Our Lady of Sorrows, and before long she was adopting the way of life of the Sisters, who held her in high esteem.

Here she had the time and facilities she needed for study; and what she chose to study was the work of St Thomas Aquinas. Her subsequent writings on St Thomas made such an impact on the Roman Catholic world that she was besieged to give lectures, and won a new fame as a speaker and Catholic writer.

This was her life for the next five years, while beneath it all she yearned for betrothal to Christ and the life of exclusive devotion to him in a contemplative's convent. But every time she spoke of this singular desire to Canon Schwind his only answer was 'the time is not yet ripe'.

The maturing of her Faith in Christ

In September 1927 Canon Schwind died. And we can again see the influence of God in the new confessor who was to guide her along the next phase of the path to perfection.

It happened like this. At Easter, 1928 Edith went to spend Holy Week at the Benedictine Abbey of Beuron. The abbey was noted for the prominent part it was playing in the liturgical movement of the time. Its abbot was Father Raphael Walzer, and he at once became her new spiritual director.

From Abbot Raphael we receive a 'first impression' which gives a startling measure of the process of conversion. In the seven years since she had become a Catholic, Edith Stein, had so nourished herself on God's graces and so submitted to his guidance that Abbot Raphael could record:

'I have seldom met a soul which united so many excellent qualities – she was simplicity and naturalness personified. She was completely a woman, gentle and even maternal without ever wanting to mother any one. Gifted with mystical graces, in the true sense of the word, she never gave any sign of affectation or a sense of superiority. She was simple with simple people, learned with the learned, yet without presumption, an enquirer with enquirers and, I would like to add, a sinner with sinners.'

Another monk, Father Zahringer, was given the gift of seeing her soul, it would seem, for he wrote:

'When I saw her for the first time in a corner of the entrance to Beuron her appearance and attitude made an impression on me which I can only compare with that of the pictures of the *Ecclesia Orans* (the praying Church) in the oldest ecclesiastical art of the Catacombs. And this was no mere chance fancy. She was in truth a type of that *Ecclesia* standing in the world of time and yet apart from it, and knowing nothing else, in the depths of her union with Christ, but the Lord's words: "For them do I sanctify myself, that they also may be sanctified in truth."'

At ground level, Edith continued her duties as teacher and was kept busy travelling in response to mounting demands for her lectures, additionally burning much midnight oil writing essays on her fresh insights into old truths.

For two years she was thus occupied, while everything in her craved to leave it all and give herself solely to Christ in the contemplative isolation of a Discalced Carmelite convent. During the Christmas of 1930 Edith was at Beuron, and she again approached her Confessor, the Abbot, about entering the Religious Order. Like Canon Schwind, Abbot Raphael was to advise that 'the time had not yet come to take such a step' – and urged her, instead, to use her great talents 'in giving lectures and in literary work for the Glory of God and in the cause of Catholic Truth.'

Throughout 1931 and well into 1932 she gave lectures arranged by Catholic colleges and societies all over Germany and Switzerland. In the spring of '32 she moved in with the Sisters of Notre Dame who ran the Collegium Marianum at Münster. Here again we have a 'first impression' which provides some evidence of the holiness which was developing within. One of the student nuns wrote:

'In spite of her frail constitution Edith Stein kept a strict fast even when engaged in strenuous intellectual work. She already practised monastic asceticism. If she could arrange it so that she could hear three Masses in succession, she could be seen throughout them all kneeling reverently upright, never leaning, never sitting.'

Or again, a Swiss woman who frequently went into one of the churches Edith used, wrote: 'She would pray for hours before Our Lady of Sorrows, I could never understand it... but now (years later with hindsight) I have come to think that Edith Stein not only prayed to have sufferings, but also had intimations that she would travel the road of suffering.'

The desire to suffer for God's sake is something which, perhaps, only the very holy can comprehend. Edith Stein by now had that desire.

On her way to spend Easter with her spiritual director at Beuron, she broke her journey at Cologne on Holy

Thursday to make the Holy Hour at the Carmelite Convent in that town. Of that hour, she wrote:

'I spoke to Our Saviour and told him that I knew that it was his cross which was now being laid on the Jewish people. Most of them did not understand it; but those who did understand must accept it willingly in the name of all. I wanted to do that; let him only show me how. When the service was over I had an interior conviction that I had been heard. But in what the bearing of the cross was to consist I did not yet know.' 'The Cross' she wanted to bear was to be an oblation of herself for the salvation of the Jewish people.

We are now in the mid-1930s. Hitler was on the rampage, and the persecution of Jews was gaining momentum. The awesome reality of the persecution of Jews through the centuries and particularly of Hitler's crescendo of vileness against her people was seen by Edith Stein in clear perspective. Her intense love for Christ was permeated with a profound sorrow and pity for her race – and her burning desire to take a share in his suffering is perhaps the key to the persistent moves in our time for her canonisation.

But even now she was not ready for the enclosed life. She resumed her journey to Beuron, and there asked Abbot Walzer if the time had not yet come when she could enter Carmel. Once again she was dissuaded.

However, conditions in Nazi Germany were bringing a new urgency to her desires, and when she returned to Münster it was to find that the director of the college had received orders from the Nazis that Dr Stein must discontinue her lectures.

The Catholic Teachers' Union undertook to take charge of her maintenance, but she was to be led along another road. About ten days after her suspension as a lecturer, she went to Münster's Church of St Luger for the thirteen hours of prayer devoted to the Feast of the Good Shepherd. She went straight up to Christ in the tabernacle and told him: 'I will not leave till I see clearly whether I may now enter Carmel.'

The flooding of her soul with his consent came as the last blessing was being given. She left the church and immediately set about arranging an interview with the Prioress of the Discalced Carmelite Convent at Cologne.

Again, she met with resistance – the Prioress, at the interview, was reluctant to accept the responsibility of taking out of the world one whose fame and intellectual brilliance had so much to offer mankind, to which Edith replied: 'It is not human activity that can help us but the Passion of Christ. It is a share in that, that I desire.'

A Discalced Carmelite at last

On the 15th April 1934 Edith Stein became a bride of Christ, and with the habit of Our Lady of Mount Carmel she retained the name Teresa – 'that she may receive the patronage of the great Saint of Avila' – and Benedicta, in gratitude to the graces she received in the Benedictine Abbey of Beuron. 'Of the Cross' was added, from her free desire to share in her Lord's sufferings.

In May, 1936, Sister Teresa Benedicta of the Cross received word that her mother was dying. Frau Stein, in the event, lingered through the summer, and on 14th September, the Feast of the Exaltation of the Cross, when the whole Discalced Carmelite Order renews its vows at one hour before dawn, her mother died. Edith wrote: 'As I was standing in my place in choir waiting to renew my vows my mother was beside me. I felt her presence quite distinctly.'

Soon after Frau Stein's death, Edith experienced great joy when her sister Rosa told her that she, too, wanted to be converted to Christ. Edith had prayed much for her sister, and religion had been discussed whenever the sisters met. Rosa had known a desire for the faith for some time, but she had held back in deference to their much-loved mother. Now, she took formal instruction, and as soon as she had arranged the family affairs, she was received into the Church at Cologne on Christmas Eve 1936, making he first Communion at Midnight Mass.

By now, the Nazis' persecution of Jews was in full flood, as well as attacks on all things sacred, including convents and monasteries The nuns feared for Sister Teresa Benedicta, and secretly made arrangements to have her transferred to the Carmelite Convent at Echt in Holland.

But Sister Teresa Benedicta's spirituality had moved, by now, to a high mystical level. This is reflected in a note she scribbled on the back of a postcard the night a doctor, a friend of the Convent, drove her – 'for a change of air' – in fact over the border into Holland. It reads:

'Dear Mother, I beg your Reverence's permission to offer myself to the Heart of Jesus as a sacrificial expiation for the sake of true peace: that the Anti-Christ's sway may be broken... I am asking this today because it is already the twelfth hour. I know that I am nothing, but Jesus wills it, and he will call many more to the same sacrifice in these days'. It is dated Passion Sunday, 26th March, 1939.

In another note she wrote of the Nazi horrors being inflicted on the Jews: 'It is the shadow of the cross which is falling on my people,' she wrote. 'If only they would see this! It is the fulfilment of the curse which my people called on its own head.'

At the convent in Holland her life continued, by now buoyant in the Spirit – 'perfectly at peace in the harbour of the Divine Will', as she herself put it – her days now a constancy of contemplative prayer, strict fasting, meditation, spiritual reading, contemplation, writing and more prayer centred on a deep love of the Mass.

Reluctantly, she was from time to time dragged out of this spiritual condition by worldly intrusions. There was her concern for her sister Rosa, who had made her escape to Belgium, penniless in a strange country whose language she did not know. There was the necessary entanglement in the ways of the world to arrange Rosa's passport to Holland, and relief, no doubt, when Rosa eventually arrived at Echt in the summer of 1940. There, Rosa was given a room outside the convent enclosure, received into the Third Order of Our Lady of Mount Carmel and henceforth the two sisters spent long hours every day in prayer and contemplation in the Convent Chapel.

The Nazis close in

There was the Gestapo. In February 1941, the Discalced Carmelite and other Convents were invaded by the Gestapo who ordered all the nuns to leave at once. Many of the Sisters were frightened, and to them Sister Teresa Benedicta said: ' if we are driven out into the street, then our Lord will send his Angels to encircle us and their invisible wings will enfold us in a peace more secure than that of the highest and most solid convent walls. Certainly we ought to pray that we may be spared this experience but only with the deeply sincere addition: "Not my will but Thine be done"'.

It is evident that she drew much strength from the essential Discalced Carmelite spirituality which was her road to perfection. Through a work she was writing at this time on St John of the Cross she developed a close spiritual companionship with this great saint, and after immersing herself in his vision of the cross and his imprisonment in Toledo, she wrote:

'To be helplessly delivered up to the wickedness of embittered enemies, tortured in body and soul, cut off from all human consolation and even from the sources of power in the sacramental life of the Church – could there be a harder school of the cross?'

She knew that she would die for Christ. Indeed, that was her desire. Had she so chosen, she may quite possibly have done otherwise, for arrangements were set under way by well-meaning friends for her and her sister Rosa to go to the safety of a Carmel in Switzerland, and if Sister Teresa Benedicta had applied herself with her customary sense of purpose to these arrangements she would almost certainly have gone there.

But she did nothing to hurry the formalities, and in May 1942 both sisters were summoned to appear before the Gestapo. When she entered the room, Sister Teresa Benedicta greeted her Nazi interrogators with the words: 'Praised be Jesus Christ'. Coming from one they saw as a Jewess, this apparently bemused the Gestapo men. When they got over it they roughly demanded identity cards, shouted that they were not in order, and subjected the sisters to a pitiless examination... then let them go back to their Convent.

For three months nothing happened, then on 2nd August, 1942, uniformed men burst into the Convent and arrested the sisters. They were given ten minutes to pack, and when they were roughly bustled into the police van they found other victims already there. It transpired that all 'non-Aryan' members of every Dutch religious community were arrested that day, as a reprisal for a pastoral letter from the Archbishop of Utrecht which had been read in all Roman Catholic churches protesting against the treatment of the Jews.

The police van took them to a transit camp at Amersfoort. Three days later the nuns back in the convent received information that the sisters were at Westerbroke camp and that they needed warm clothing, blankets and medicine. Amid tears and prayers the community made up parcels, and two men who delivered them were able, by the courtesy of the Dutch police, to talk to the sisters in private. Sister Teresa Benedicta told them that there were ten nuns in their hut and that the German Commandant had ordered that the Catholic Jews be isolated from the non-Catholics.

'Sister Teresa Benedicta was perfectly calm and composed,' the two men reported. 'She was happy that she was able to help and comfort the prisoners by words and prayer. Her deep faith created about her an atmosphere of confidence, and she said: 'Whatever happens I am prepared for it; our dear Child Jesus is with us.' Rosa was also bearing up well, encouraged and strengthened by her sister's example.'

Two days later, on 7th August, one of her former pupils waiting on the station platform at Schifferstadt heard her name being called from a slowly passing train. She recognised the voice of her old Professor, Doktor Stein: 'Give my love to the Sisters of St Magdalena's; I am travelling eastwards.' 'Eastwards' was a euphemism for the concentration camp (Auschwitz), the gas chamber and death.

She was never heard of again.

The most reliable information is that she and her sister were gassed on the 9th or 10th August 1942, and their bodies burned.

When Sister Teresa Benedicta's cell was cleared out a small picture was found with her handwriting on the back. It read: 'I wish to offer my life as a sacrifice for the conversion of the Jews.'

Beatification and Canonisation

Edith Stein was beatified on 1st May 1987 by Pope John Paul II during his second pastoral visit to Germany. The beatification took place in the vast Müngersdorf football stadium in Cologne. Amid great celebrations, and even some controversy, she was canonized by Pope John Paul II in Rome on 11th October 1998. The whole church celebrates her feast day on 9th August: St Edith Stein, Teresa Benedicta of the Cross.

MARCEL CALLO

by
M. N. L. Couve de Murville
Archbishop of Birmingham

Early Life

In 1987 Pope John Paul II solemnly beatified a young Frenchman, Marcel Callo, and said of him "the whole of his life became a Eucharist". Marcel had died in a Nazi concentration camp. No greater contrast can be imagined: the great religious ceremony in the marble splendour of St Peter's, bringing together Bishops from all over the world for the Synod on the Laity, and what we know about Marcel's miserable end in isolation, degradation and pain.

Marcel Callo came from Rennes, in Western France, the capital of Brittany; his father and mother had been born in a rural part of the province, in the Morbihan district, and they had both come to Rennes in search of work. Monsieur Callo, who had been in the French army during the First World War, had a small job in the Highways Department. Madame Callo, after two years schooling, had started work at the age of eleven at the local chateau at Peillac and learnt the superb French tradition of home cooking. Then she came to Rennes and worked in domestic service. They were married in 1919 and had eight children. The eldest, Jean, later became a priest. Marcel was the second child, born on 6th December 1921 and baptised in the Church of St Aubin.

The family was poor but not destitute. They first lived in rented accommodation; later Monsieur Callo was able to benefit from the provisions of the 1928 Loi Loucheur which helped workers to acquire their own homes. He obtained a loan from the State, repayable over twenty years, to buy an old house. While it was being restored, the family lived in a basement and Marcel said: "We lived one winter like baby Jesus in the crib". The Callo house at 8 rue des Tanneurs. still stands and is a "two-up and two-down" with the front door opening straight into the kitchen-living room. Next to it on the ground floor was the parents' bedroom. Upstairs there was one room for the boys and one for the girls. In the yard at the back were the lavatories and a room where they washed in tubs, with hot water brought in from the kitchen.

The family were strongly Catholic and had a profound respect for the clergy at St Aubin's Church, which was only ten minutes walk away; Jean and Marcel served Mass every morning. In the evening, family prayers were quite an event. The father went to bed early because he got up at 5.00.a.m. to light the fires in the Highways Department Office. He would make the sign of the cross on the fore-heads of his children before going to his room and they would see him kneeling at the foot of the bed, surely one of the most effective religious lessons that a child ever receives. The rest of the family gathered in the living room and said the Rosary out loud, during which the children finished the washing up and put things away while the mother was darning clothes. Then everyone would kneel down and recite together the set form of night prayers.

Marcel made his Solemn First Communion at the age of ten and a half in the parish Church, having made a Private Communion at the Convent of the Adoration when he was seven. The more festive occasion at a later age, which was popular with families and ensured that children attended catechism class regularly between the two events. Confirmation came for Marcel in 1933 when he was twelve years old.

The boys went to school at the parish primary school where the two curates of St Aubin were teachers. It was a paying school and the parents had to find the fees from their meagre income. For a time Marcel was in the Scouts, but eventually he had to give this up because the family could not afford the cost of the uniform and of the camps. Marcel, with the emotiveness that came from his Breton ancestry, shed a tear or two over this. In 1932 Jean decided that he wanted to be a priest and went to the Diocesan Junior Seminary at the age of twelve; fortunately he benefited from a bursary so that his studies all the way to the priesthood did not cost his parents anything.

Printer

In those days education in France was only compulsory
until the age of thirteen. Marcel left school in the summer of
1934, his thirteenth year, and began work as a printer's
apprentice on 1st October. His parents had consulted the
clergy about suitable employment for their son and were
recommended to apply to the printing works owned by
Eugene Delahaye, who was well in with the ecclesiastical
establishment of the city.

Marcel suffered throughout his life from abdominal pain,
often acute, and this was probably caused by lead poisoning
at the printing works.

Marcel's entry into working life came as a great shock to
him, firstly because of the attitude towards religion on the
part of his fellow workers. Whatever Monsieur Delahaye's
relation to the Church may have been, it certainly had no
influence on his employees. The dominant attitude in the
shop, where people talked freely while working, was one of
cordial hatred of the clergy, les curés as they were called.
Marcel, who had lived in the atmosphere of a practising
Catholic family up till then, was shaken to discover that he
was immediately marked out as a Church-goer. People had
no time for the Church because they thought it did not care
for the working class and was in league with those who
exploited it.

The other thing that shook Marcel was the way people
talked about sex. They seemed to take great pleasure in

making explicit references to their performance in this
domain and observing the effect on the apprentice boys
who were just out of school. Some of the women were the
worst and habitually used the crudest language. It was all
upsetting for Marcel who had so much been looking forward to earning a little money so as to help out his parents;
not that the pay of an apprentice came to very much. He
earned 1.50 francs a day at a time when tobacco cost 3.50
francs for a packet of 40 grams. It was an eight hour day,
from 8.15.a.m. to midday and from 2.00.p.m. to 6.15.p.m.
Marcel worked standing which he found very tiring at first.
He learnt to compose type, picking out the letters one by
one from the compartments in the type cases and making up
the lines of print which were then locked into place in metal
frames called "chases".

Young Christian Worker

At this difficult time, Marcel found support in a group
which had been started in the parish of St Aubin by Fr Jules
Martinais. They were the Young Christian Workers
(Jeunesse Ouvrière Chrétienne or JOC, the members being
called *Jocistes*). Fr Martinais, who was known familiarly as
p'tit Jules, had a wonderful way with young people. Behind
the presbytery in the Rue Saint Louis was a small courtyard
and a range of buildings with meeting rooms. The curate
installed a Ping-pong table and encouraged youngsters to
drop in. There was not much going on in the evening in

Rennes, so they came. After a time *p'tit Jules* gave them the idea of meeting in smaller groups so as to discuss the Catholic faith and to think about its bearing on their life at work. This is exactly what Marcel needed. The JOC had been founded by a Belgian priest, Joseph Cardijn, in 1912. Fr Cardijn, who later became a Cardinal, had devised a system for preventing group discussions from remaining mere talk by a method called "see – judge – act". He wanted young workers firstly to take stock of the conditions of work and of society; secondly, to decide what could be done practically to change things for the better; and thirdly, to set themselves an attainable goal of action at one meeting which could be reported on at the next. The method was brilliant in its simplicity and it was also applied to the group-study of the New Testament, so that reading the Gospels and meditating on them became second nature to *Jocistes*. With this method went an organisation similar to that of the Communist Party, whereby delegates from the weekly section meetings met monthly in Provincial Councils, and provided other delegates to meet in a National Council. Reports and directives could travel up and down this simple but effective network.

At the printing works, Marcel had been joined in 1941 by another apprentice typographer, Roger Renoncet. Roger noticed the way the other workers respected Marcel. Of course, they tried to shock Roger when he arrived, just as they had done with Marcel. Once, when a man said something particularly objectionable, Marcel said: "How would you like it if I spoke like that in front of your kids?", and the man shut up. When Marcel went down to the print room with the heavy chases of newsprint, Roger noticed that people minded their language. That was strange because Marcel was so young. There was something about him that people respected. He wanted workers to respect each other because he believed in their intrinsic worth, and somehow that had an effect. Of course, they still pulled his leg and referred to him sometime as "Jesus Christ". His usual nickname was Mikado, because he had a round face, thick glasses for long-sightedness and half closed eyes when he laughed.

Marcel persuaded Roger to join the JOC group at St Aubin. Together they planned an open witness to faith for Good Friday. At three o'clock they turned off the electricity in the printing works and called for one minute's silence to honour the time of Jesus' death on the cross. People were so surprised that they obeyed. Another time Marcel and the JOC group debated how to observe All Saints Day, which is a public holiday in France. Because it is a great festival of the Church, they considered that it should be a joyful occasion and so they decided to go to the cinema. The pious ladies of the parish were scandalised because in France the afternoon of All Saints was the time for visiting family graves and for the First Vespers of All Souls, when St Aubin's was draped in black and everyone was expected to be gloomy.

Roger was impressed by Marcel's attitude to the Mass; it meant so much to him. Although he could not go to Mass every day, he usually tried to attend once in the week. The JOC would talk about the readings of the Sunday Mass and prepare it together; learning new songs and hymns was an important part of their religious life. Marcel gave the group the idea of offering Mass for a particular intention when they went, just as the priest does; Roger commented: "It changed me from being a spectator into something else". When war broke out in September 1939, the JOC group decided that every day of the week one of its members would go to Mass and communion; Marcel saw to it that the rota was kept up.

Marcel's work experience and his commitment to the evangelisation of the working class was helping him to mature, but his emotional support still came from his family. The understanding of the parents for one another and their unity were the background to the development of their eight children.

Because his poor mother was so tired looking after the little ones, Marcel would spend his Saturday morning doing the housework and having a major clean-out; he did not go to work on Saturday and it would have been a temptation for him either to lie in bed or to have a good time, but he put the support of his mother first. The younger children would be organised by him as part of the operation of cleaning the house from top to bottom. Sometimes they resented it and thought their older brother very "bossy". There was also a special ritual on Sundays at their home. Madame Callo would go to the early Mass at 6.30; when she came back, her husband and the children went to the 10 o'clock Mass while she prepared the Sunday lunch. After lunch everyone went to see Jean at the seminary, except Marcel who stayed at home and did all the washing up himself. Afterwards he went down to the Rue Saint Louis and was at his meeting until late at night.

Marguerite

Marcel was meticulous about everything and he was careful about his appearance, which could be described as dapper. When off work, he often wore a suit and tie; his hair was smarmed down with haircream, in the way that was popular among men at the time. When he was twenty Marcel began to think of marriage and starting his own home. Towards the end of 1941 he had met a girl called Marguerite Derniaux when they were both on an outside collection for French Prisoners of War in Germany. She worked at the Post Office and her parents, who were rather possessive of their only child, owned a cafe-restaurant. It seems to have been love at first sight. By the end of 1942 they were unofficially engaged. They looked forward to a big celebration in the summer when they would announce their engagement publicly. But Marcel never did marry or found a home. In 1943 he entered his own Way of the Cross which was to take him away from all those he loved and to end in his early death, aged only twenty-three.

Call-Up

The war also caught up with Rennes through allied bombing. On the 8th March 1943 American Flying Fortresses flying high bombed the railway station in full daylight and some of the bombs fell on office buildings nearby where Marie Madeleine, the eldest of the Callo sisters, was working. Marcel was in the printing works when news of what had happened spread through the city; he rushed down to the station and started helping the rescue services to clear the rubble. In fact he was the one who discovered the dead body of his sister. In a state of shock, he went back home to break the news to his parents. The family was grief-stricken. Marie Madeleine was buried on 10th March and that very day Marcel showed his brother the call-up papers for the STO that he had received. He said "Jean, what do I do about this?"

The days of grieving for Marie Madeleine overshadowed for the Callo family the implications of Marcel's imminent departure; anyway, they hoped he would eventually come back and there were periods of leave to look forward to. For Marcel however the weeks before he left for Germany was a time of anxious soul-searching. He did not want to leave Marguerite when they had just got engaged and were looking forward to getting married; nor did he want to work for the hated Nazi regime at a time when opposition to it was becoming possible. Many young men evaded their call-up by going underground; some joined the Resistance Movement and it would have been possible for Marcel to hide with his Breton relatives near Redon in the Morbihan and to do the same. But there were other considerations. There was the fear of reprisals against his father or his brother if he failed to turn up. Jean was due to be ordained priest in June. What if the police sent him forcibly to Germany instead?

There was also the sense of responsibility on the part of the JOC for French workers in Germany. Was it not the duty of a Christian worker to be with them and to exercise his apostolate among them? After anxious days and nights of reflection, Marcel decided that it was his duty to go. He said to one of his aunts: "I'm going as a missionary, you know". On his last day in Rennes, 19th March 1943, he said goodbye to his family and to Marguerite at home. He asked them not to go down to the station with him because he felt the parting there would be too painful. Jacques Mahieu, a fellow Jociste, came to carry his bag: so they went both of them together, past the Church of St Aubin and down the Rue Saint Louis where Marcel had so often gone to the JOC meetings. One wonders if he had a presentiment that he would never see any of it again.

Thuringia

Marcel was sent to the eastern German province of Thuringia, to a small town called Zella-Mehlis. He was allocated to the *Carl Walther Waffenfabrik* which employed 1,500 German workers and had 1,000 foreign workers, mostly French and Belgians. There were in all about 7,000 foreign workers in Zella-Mehlis from seventeen different nationalities.

Marcel worked at the assembly of rocket-firing pistols. His working day lasted 10 to 11 hours with an hour off for lunch. The German workers had better food than the foreigners, whose diet was mostly potatoes and cabbage. The housing conditions for the foreign workers were also poor; they were crowded in bunks in wooden huts. The purchasing power of their wages was very limited and they had no legal status in Germany and nowhere to turn for redress if they were badly treated at work.

At first there was a prospect of leave in France; Marcel was designated to go home in June 1943. He looked forward to attending the first communion of two of his sisters and the ordination of Jean to the priesthood. He also intended to announce his engagement to Marguerite, but his leave depended on the return of one of his fellow workers. Since the man never came back from France, Marcel was not allowed to go. All home leave was cancelled anyway after the spring of 1944.

During the first two months, Marcel almost broke down. He reproached himself for making the wrong decision and not trying to evade his call-up. He was very homesick. Having never been away from home for any length of time, he missed his family and his fiancee terribly. He suffered from the attitude of the other men in the camp, from the gross materialism and immorality. He felt diminished by being forced to work for the Nazi cause and in conditions assigned to him by those who considered themselves as a master race. He wrote home a lot during his first month in Germany and his letters gave evidence of the way in which he reacted to the challenge. The key phrase is "I soon realised that the best way to cheer up and keep going was to forget one's own misery and to think of everyone else's". Marcel remembered why he had decided to come to Germany, to be a missionary among the other French workers. The first thing was to discover other members of the JOC in the camp and to agree to meet and pray, however tired they might feel at the end of the day. He also discovered that there was a Catholic Church at Zella-Mehlis.

By the time Easter 1943 came round, Marcel had worked on the other eighteen men in his room so that all but one went to Mass. The curate who came from Suhl, Fr Steinberg, spoke French; Marcel prevailed on him to arrange special Masses for French-speaking foreign workers and these began in September and were celebrated once or twice a month on Sunday afternoon. The hymns were in

French and Marcel said a few words at the end of the celebration. He was so pleased because there were over a hundred workers at the first Mass, some of whom had not been to Church for years.

Morale

The JOC group put their mind to other ways of restoring the morale of their fellow workers. They organised a football team and Marcel wrote home that they felt good at having beaten the Czech team. They staged plays; people had nothing to read, so the *Jocistes* organised a lending library by asking their families to send books from France. In addition, like Frenchmen the world over, Marcel and his friends knew the importance of the meal as an expression of civilisation. They would buy some bottles of wine and prepare a special meal that they could enjoy at weekends; that did wonders for morale but Marcel saved most of his pay so that he could remit it regularly to his family.

Marcel was part of a network of Catholic groups which was created secretly in Thuringia. Young Christian workers, Scouts and seminarians made contact with one another and did what they could for their fellow workers.

Not only were there over 700 *Jocistes* among the STO workers; soon many priests were working among them too. More than 300 priests in all were able to do some apostolic work among the 700,000 or so French forced workers in Germany. They began to make contact with active Jocistes on the factory floor, to distribute communion and celebrate Mass secretly, to hear confessions.

By the autumn of 1943 the Gestapo knew that the camps of French workers in Germany were infiltrated by what they considered to be subversive Catholic Action. Having banned Catholic Action in Germany when they seized power in 1933, the Nazis were particularly riled at seeing it raise its head deep in their own country under what they imagined to be the directive of a foreign prelate. During the autumn and winter of 1943 they were collecting information, ready to pounce so as to eradicate the poison of Catholic social work from the sacred soil of the Fatherland. The *Jocistes* knew they were being watched but this did not stop them from continuing with their meetings. In a letter of 24th January 1944, Marcel wrote: "an excellent day which gives one fresh courage but which was not without its difficulties and which gave us a few nasty shocks. You understand, don't you. I needn't say more".

Arrests

For Himmler and his SS, the Catholic Church was always a prime target. Several hundred German priests had been arrested for their opposition to the Hitler regime. A circular of June 1943 had forbidden German priests to put on special Masses for foreign workers. The first arrests among unauthorised priests working with French workers took place in the summer of 1943. Priests and seminarians who were without authorisation were either sent back to France or interned in concentration camps. On 3rd December 1943 a decree was promulgated which banned Catholic apostolate of any sort among French workers in Germany. Soon more searches and arrests followed. On 21st January 1944 Himmler ordered that all seminarians who had come to Germany as part of the French labour force should be identified and deported. In April 1944 the Gestapo was ready to strike in Thuringia. A list of names and addresses of the JOC section leaders was found when the brothers André and Roger Vallée were searched at Gotha. Marcel's name was on the list; on 19th April he was arrested. When the Gestapo man came into the hut to search all Marcel's belongings, another Frenchman asked why he was being taken away. He was told scornfully: "this gentleman is far too Catholic". There could be no doubt about the motive for his arrest and eventual death.

Interrogation

Marcel was taken to the neighbouring town of Gotha where he was interrogated by the Gestapo together with other *Jocistes* and a priest of the Diocese of Rennes, Fr Jean Lecoq, indicted for having said Mass. They admitted that they were members of a Catholic youth group but denied that they had any links with political resistance to the regime. On 27th April they were transferred to the town gaol to await the judgement of their case by Gestapo headquarters in Berlin. This was a secret administrative process with no recourse of any kind to public courts and no possibility of defence. In fact they did not receive their sentence until 25th September. The *Jocistes* were put into prison cells and were taken out daily to work as navvies or farm labourers. Many prisoners of war were at work in the farms too and there were opportunities for smuggling out letters through them and also for receiving messages and food from the other *Jocistes* in the work camps, who had continued their secret organisation in spite of the known danger. Marcel was not well during this time and had a lot of stomach pain, probably due to lead contamination when he was a printer. The prison food was insufficient for manual labourers. He suffered an outbreak of painful boils but in his letters home he tried to be positive. He commented that, because they were locked up early after the evening meal, he was enjoying *une cure de sommeil*, "a course of sleep therapy"!

While they were in prison at Gotha, they were only able to receive Holy Communion once. Local *Jocistes* asked the parish priest to give them hosts that they could convey to the prisoners secretly but he refused. He had been in serious trouble with the Gestapo for having allowed Fr Lecoq to say Mass in his parish Church and he considered that it was too dangerous to take more risks. However, Marcel, who noted on the back of an old newspaper the dates as they passed during their time in prison, was able to write under 16th July, 1944 "Communion. Immense joy!". It was probably the last time that Marcel Callo received his Lord in Communion.

Letters From Prison

Marcel's letters to his family from prison give us an insight into his spirituality. The first one was a card written in pencil on 13th May 1944. His main concern is that his family will be shattered to learn where he is, so he tries to reassure them although he cannot allude directly to prison, since the card was posted from Zella-Mehlis and was presumably taken back there by one of his friends:

"At last I can write to you as I feel less weak. When I left I asked my mates to write to you, I am sure they have done this, so you know how my accident occurred, I was expecting it. Don't worry about me I am well. I am in a boarding-house like the one cousin Michel was in for a time [his first cousin Michel had been put in prison for a time in Rennes by the Germans]. The food is good but there is not enough of it unfortunately, I go out now and again to work, the work is heavy... My dear parents don't cry and whatever you do don't pity me, let's offer it all to the Lord, every day I offer all my troubles for you, for my future home, for my dear JOC; pray for me that Christ may always be with me, that I may always be in good spirits as I am now. Next time I will write to my little Marguerite, let's all be brave, let's put all our trust in Christ and his holy mother".

He ended the card *Vive le Christ!*

On 6th July 1944 Marcel wrote:

"I haven't had any news at all from you, from my friends or from my mates for three months. I feel really alone at times and I can't hide my sorrow. I was used to getting so many letters from you and my little Marguerite that this lack of letters leaves a big gap; still, I haven't given up hope of having news from you soon. Fortunately there's a Friend who doesn't leave me for a moment. He knows how to keep me going and to cheer me up when I feel that things are just too hard; when he is there one can put up with anything; how grateful I am to Christ for having led me on the way that I am going now; it's great to be able to offer him days like these; how my daily offering must please him; I offer up all my sufferings and hardship for all of you, for you my very dear Parents, for my little Fiancée, for Jean, that his priestly ministry may be fruitful, for all my friends and mates, yes it really is a joy and it makes me feel good to be able to suffer for those I love.

There is one thing I worry about more and more and which makes me feel sad, I am afraid that one day you will be in the fighting zone. I beg Christ to spare you and I ask Our Lady to protect you; that's my daily prayer. Every night before I go to sleep I think of the future; I think of what's good in me and of what's bad, I try to become better and to grow nearer and nearer to God; I am gradually preparing to build the super home that I am going to have with Marguerite when I get back; I also think every night

about France; how I would like to see it doing well; I and
all my mates here, we feel bad at seeing our country in the
state it is in now; all of us who have been through it here,
we want to build France up again and to make it the great
place it should be. Three things go together: God, Family,
Homeland, and they should never be separated; if everyone
would build on that and make it a basis for their action
everything would be alright. My very dear parents, I feel I
wanted to talk about all these things tonight, I feel better for
having written like that; I have forgotten my sorrow for a
bit."

In this letter Marcel alludes to the fighting which followed the Allied landing in Normandy on 6th June. On 4th
August 1944, the American armoured columns entered
Rennes and after that there could be no more communica-
tion between Marcel and his family.

"The Church"

On 5th August 1944 the political prisoners in the Gotha
gaol were put together in a larger cell on the second floor of
the prison; it was called *die Kirche*, "the Church", because
the Lutheran chaplain had used it to hold services. It had
five windows and a view of the street below. Roger Vallée
called it "the Upper Room" and it was truly inhabited by
twelve disciples of the Lord. As well as Fr Lecoq there
were three seminarians, Jean Tinturier of the diocese of
Bourges, Roger Vallée of the diocese of Sées and a Jesuit

Scholastic, Paul Beschet. The eight *Jocistes* included Marcel, Roger Vallée's brother André and Marcel Carrier, from Saint-Ouen, near Paris, an older man married with children, who had been the JOC Federal Leader for Thuringia.

After the day's work, it was good to be together and to share as they had been used to do. They arranged the mattresses from the bunk beds round the table so that they could have their meals in common; they shared everything they had been able to collect during the day, cigarettes and any food passed to them by local *Jocistes*. One of them made a cross out of dried flowers and this was fixed prominently to the wall. They were also given a Missal and two New Testaments. On Sundays they would read the Mass texts, though Fr Lecoq was never able to celebrate the Mass itself. Jean Tinturier would prepare a talk on the Gospels for Fridays. Fr Lecoq would hear their confessions and they would also practice a public accusation of faults during their daily evening prayer. It was like a community of the early Christians. Sometimes the prison warders opened the spy-hole to look into the cell and were astounded to see these young men kneeling and saying the Rosary. It was a glimpse into another world.

Of that group, only four were to return to France, Fr Lecoq, Fr Beschet and two Jocistes, René Le Tonquèze and Fernand Morin. All the others perished in Nazi concentration camps. On 25th September their sentence came from

Berlin. Each one was judged guilty of the following crime: "because of his Catholic action among his French comrades during his obligatory work service he constituted a threat to the State and to the German people".

On 8th October 1944 Marcel Callo left the Gotha prison with ten of his fellow prisoners, bound for the concentration camps to which they had been condemned. Meanwhile, the war pursued its course. Paris had been freed by the Allies on 25th August 1944 and General de Gaulle attended a great service of Thanksgiving in Notre Dame. In February 1945 Germany was invaded. The Allies crossed the Rhine in early March. On 25th April the Russians reached the out-skirts of Berlin, where Hitler committed suicide in his underground bunker on 30th April. On the 7th May 1945 the German Armed Forces surrendered unconditionally to the Allies. All this was welcome news to the French people who had suffered four years of German occupation, but for the Callo family there was no news; only the anguish of not knowing what had happened to Marcel. They hoped against hope that he was still alive and would come back one day.

Then at the beginning of June 1945 a former Colonel of the French Army knocked at the door of the Callo home. He was called Albert Tibodo and he lived in Rennes. Unfortunately M. and Mme. Callo were not at home. Colonel Tibodo left the neighbours his address and told them that he had been with Marcel when he died at the con-centration camp of Mauthausen. So he was dead then! By

evening the whole neighbourhood knew, but no one dared
to tell the parents. The next day Fr Jean Callo went to see
Colonel Tibodo and it was he who finally broke the news to
the family. Tibodo had only been with Marcel during the
last few hours of his earthly existence, so he could not say
anything about the time between Marcel's last letter in July
1944 and his death on the 19th March 1945. A priest from
Rennes, Fr Jean Baptiste Jégo, C.J.M., who knew the Callo
family, collected information from some of the priests who
had been in the concentration camps at Flossenburg and
Mauthausen and who survived to return to France. He
wrote a book called *Un Exemple: Marcel Callo 1921–1945*
which was published in 1946. As a result two other people
who had been with Marcel contacted the family. One of
them was Daniel Bonino who was in a sanatorium in
Lyons, having contracted tuberculosis in Germany. He
came to Rennes to see the family and gave them a lot of
details on the terrible existence in the camps. The other was
Dr Jean Peissel a Frenchman who had been a doctor at
Mauthausen and examined Marcel shortly before he died.
From these witnesses gradually the outline of Marcel's last
months could be made out.

Concentration Camp

Concentration camps were a hideous concomitant of the
Nazi regime. They sought to degrade their inmates by
means of malnutrition, overcrowding and overwork. The

organisation of the camps was in the hands of the SS, the special Nazi force under Himmler which was like a state within the State. The labour camps provided income for the SS and all details of the organisation were controlled by SS headquarters in Berlin.

The actual running of the overcrowded wooden huts was left by the SS to Kapos, often common law criminals who were Poles, Czechs, Russians or Ukrainians. The Kapos curried favour with the SS by treating the convicts brutally. Beatings were frequent. Roll calls, lasting for hours sometimes, kept the prisoners standing in rows, often in freezing temperatures, sometimes in the middle of the night. Gradually the morale of the convicts was destroyed by a combination of starvation, ill treatment and hopelessness.

Marcel was sent, manacled to four other convicts, to the concentration camp at Flossenburg, then, at the end of October, to Mauthausen near Linz. There the prisoners worked in a vast underground factory for the manufacture of Messerschmitt planes. Marcel, in an exhausted state, had to do a heavy welding job. In February 1945 someone stole his glasses; peering at his work because of long-sightedness caused him constant strain. His eyes became terribly bloodshot as a result. By then he had lost everything that he could call his own – the small prayer book that he had hidden in the mattress of his bunk-bed, the fragments of letters and photos of Marguerite that he had secreted in his shoes, all these were stolen by other prisoners. But he was still con-

cerned about the morale of his fellow sufferers. Bonino
remembers that he would say to them: "Do not give up.
God watches over us." Sometimes when they were carrying
material down long corridors, they could pause in a corner,
out of sight of the guards, and Marcel would start the Hail
Mary. He would say: "Have confidence; Christ is with us".
But Marcel could express his anguish too; Bonino remembers him saying: "How inhuman it all is! No beast on earth
is treated with such beastliness".

Tuberculosis and typhus were rife in these camps. The
convicts who had to provide long hours of work were weak
with malnutrition, yet any mistake on the assembly line was
treated as sabotage. The culprit had to strip and to receive
twenty-five blows from a Gummi, a rubber truncheon. Four
times Marcel had to undergo this punishment. In spite of all
his suffering, Bonino reports that Marcel never insulted his
tormentors. Once, when Bonino swore at them in the
foulest terms, Marcel stopped him short. This tiny detail
gives us an insight into Marcel's inner strength. He never
allowed hatred to find a place in his heart.

On 5th January 1945 Marcel collapsed and spent a fort-
night in the infirmary. It meant transferring from one kind
of torture to another. Dr Peissel writing later on the conditions in the infirmary said this: "I remember seeing your
brother and treating him... he had a pulmonary condition
(tuberculosis?) which I could not diagnose accurately
because of the lack of means of medical examination at our

disposal. Towards the end, his condition was complicated by the current dysentery which was not a disease in itself but a symptom of wasting and starvation" (Letter of Dr Peissel to Abbé Jean Callo, 20th March, 1946). Dr Peissel wrote again: "Your mention of Tibodo prompted further reminiscences on the appearance of your brother. I alluded to the ambient physical degradation (patients five to a bed from different nationalities, killing each other, fighting at night to have a bit of space; what happened too was that the night staff would club those who were screaming with pain or who fouled their bed). Ninety-five per cent were in such conditions. Your brother was in the middle of it all but I can't remember how he died in that hell-hole, where thirty to forty patients died every day" (Letter of 30th March, 1946).

Marcel's Death

After that, there is no glimpse of Marcel until almost his last hour. This was entered in the camp register of deaths as 2.55.a.m. on 19th March, 1945. He must have been admitted to the infirmary after a further spell of work, but we do not know exactly when. Colonel Tibodo testifies to Marcel's final degradation. There was an open-air latrine outside the huts, a great pit known to the Germans as the Scheissbett. To use it one had to cling to an iron bar which was too highly placed. The sick would sometimes fall into the pit and die there. This is what nearly happened to Marcel. However Tibodo saw him and, as there were no guards around, pulled him out and carried him back to the hut. He was just a bag of bones; he weighed nothing at all and Tibodo said that he carried him as one carries a child and laid him on his bed. He was totally exhausted and almost past speech, but he managed to say three words: Marcel… Callo… Rennes. That is how Tibodo was able to contact his family afterwards.

Marcel tried to say something else but Tibodo could not make out what it was. He went to make an infusion of oak bark to relieve Marcel's dysentery; patients were forbidden from doing anything for each other, so he was taking a risk but fortunately no one saw him. When he came back Marcel was dying and unable to drink or speak; his eyes were open and there was something about the look on his face which Colonel Tibodo never forgot. He said later: "I am an old pagan (parpaillot). I have seen thousands of prisoners die, but I was struck by the look on the face of Marcel Callo because there was something really extraordinary about him. It was a revelation to me: the look on his face expressed the deep conviction that he was going towards total bliss. It was like an act of faith and hope in a better life. I have never seen anything like it anywhere else with any dying person (and I have seen thousands of them), nothing like what I saw in his gaze.

A Healer Of Memories

When the full story of the concentration camps was known after the War, there was a reaction of horror and unbelief in the West, as if it were impossible that such things could happen in our century. Then after the fall of the Communist regimes in Eastern Europe similar horrors were revealed, and again more recently after the war in the former Yugoslavia. There seems no end to man's inhumanity to man. That is why it is important that the memory of the world's victims should not be lost. Each generation needs to be told what has happened, what is happening and what can happen again in our world. The temptations of power need to be seen for what they are and the capacity for evil in the human heart must be recognised in order to be exorcised.

The Church is one of the communities entrusted with the memory of the world's victims. The Church can only proclaim the example of such victims with integrity because it knows itself to be penitent and forgiven, but by naming them it becomes a voice for the voiceless. That is one of the reasons why the cult of saints is important. As a saint of the Catholic Church, Marcel Callo will never be forgotten; his story will be told all over the world and in remote ages, as prayers are offered to God through him. All the victims of an inhuman regime are commemorated in him and in the other saints of the Nazi era: Saint Maximilian Kolbe, Saint Edith Stein, Blessed Titus Brandsma, Blessed Karl Leisner, Blessed Franz Jägerstätter...

But it is necessary to go beyond commemoration. The cult of Marcel Callo is strong in Germany where he is seen as one who intercedes for the land where he suffered martyrdom. As such he is no longer only a memory, but a healer of memories. He can help the German people to come to terms with their past. The innumerable sufferers of the Nazi regime are represented in Marcel and in the other victims who accepted to die in union with Christ, the pure victim. As victims who do not victimise they are no longer merely a terrible reproach. They can reconcile others to God. To be such a victim it is necessary not only to be killed but to forgive one's killers; that is the price of redemption. When the Pope said that Marcel's life became a Eucharist, he alluded to a death which was the consummation of a lifetime of self-offering because it identified Marcel with the One who prayed on the Cross for his enemies.

TITUS BRANDSMA

by
Hugh Clarke

Introduction

It was about six o'clock on the evening of 19th January 1942. Two men knocked on the door of the Carmelite priory in Nijmegen, Holland, and asked for Fr Titus Brandsma. After a long conversation conducted in German Titus led one of the two men into his bedroom, where they were found by the prior of the house.

'This gentleman of the Sicherheitspolizei has come to arrest me,' explained Titus.

He knelt down before his young Superior and asked for a blessing. Changing his brown habit for a black suit, Titus followed his visitors to a waiting car which carried them to the railway station to catch the 6.35 p.m. train to Arnhem. That night Titus rested on a straw mattress in a prison cell; he did not sleep. The following morning he was taken by train to the Hague. He was on his way to the concentration camp of Dachau.

Early Years

Anno Sjoerd Brandsma was born on 23rd February 1881 on a large farm at Oegeklooster in Frisia, a province in the north of Holland. Cut off from the rest of the country by lakes and rivers, Frisian Catholics had always maintained a spirit of independence and resilience to new ideas. The Brandsma family had shown themselves wholehearted and active Catholics. Titus, as Anno was to call himself when he entered the Carmelite Order, took pride in his ancestry: 'I have the privilege of coming from a family in which one lived warmly with everything that advanced the cause of Frisian Catholics.'

The family consisted of four girls and two boys, all of whom except one were destined for the religious life. Theirs was a busy farm life, in the days when butter and cheese were still made on the farm itself. At school Anno showed himself intelligent and lively, yet with an independence which foreshadowed his future career. Apparently it was the custom when boys stayed behind for French lessons to share sweets with one another. On one occasion Anno decided to break with this tradition; promptly he was grabbed and held under the village pump!

Anno made his first Holy Communion at eleven, the usual age at that time, on 4th May 1892. Just before, he had intimated to his parents that he wished to become a priest, as did his brother a little later. His mother and father accepted their decision even though it meant that they would be

deprived of their help on the farm and would have to provide for their education for an extra six years.

Anno left the farm in September of that year for the
junior seminary at Megen in the southern province of
Brabant, conducted by the Franciscans. He made good
progress with his studies, being specially interested in history and literature. A good mixer, he showed himself of independent mind and was well-liked by his class-mates. Small
in stature, Anno's health gave some cause for alarm, but the
holidays spent on the farm soon restored him so that he was
able to continue his studies.

During his last year at the college he began to think
about the religious life. One of the Franciscans had told
him: 'You are too clever to become a Jesuit!' In fact neither
of these religious families attracted him; he turned towards
the Carmelite Order, whose spirituality drew him – their
spirit of prayer and special devotion to Mary the Mother of
God, whose scapular they wore. In September 1898, after
the long summer holiday, Anno made his way to Boxmeer,
where he entered the Carmelite novitiate, taking the name
of Titus at his clothing with the Carmelite habit.

Novice and Student

Seventeen years of age, good-looking and small in stature,
Titus began his novitiate. The Carmel which he entered had
been opened in 1653. It was a forbidding building and the
novitiate at that time was austere. The day began at 5.30

a.m. and ended at 8 p.m. Divine Office, Mass, meditation, spiritual reading, study, manual labour and lectures on the Carmelite Rule and way of life filled most of the day and the novices rose in the middle of the night to recite the Office of Matins. They were frequently moved from room to room; the heating was inadequate for the cold winters, which were not dissimilar from those experienced in the south of England.

Here at Boxmeer Titus with his five companions in the novitiate strove to acquire the true spirit of Carmel, the spirit of the great Old Testament prophet Elijah and of Mary, Queen and Beauty of Carmel. Life was not easy, but Titus assured his mother, when writing to her for her birthday in October 1898, that he had settled down well and asked for prayers that he might seek only the Will of God. Those who knew him use the word 'ardent' to describe his attitude during this period, but at the same time he showed himself calm and self-composed.

On 3rd October 1899 Titus made his first profession, but he remained in the novitiate for another year, as was then the custom – a little later the novitiate was reduced to one year. In the following September he began his study of philosophy; during this time he had plenty of opportunity to study the lives of the saints, especially those of Carmel. From this time dates his great love for St Teresa of Avila, the Carmelite who reformed the Order in the sixteenth century. In 1900, still only a student, he pub-

lished his Anthology drawn from the works of Saint
Teresa.

In September 1901 the Carmelite priest, Dr Hubertus
Driessen, was appointed to teach philosophy at Boxmeer;
he was to have a great influence on Titus's future. At the
very beginning of the course a problem arose because of the
professor's Latin pronunciation: none of the students could
understand him! Titus offered to act as mediator; the result
was that Dr Hubertus, who took the intervention in good
part, agreed to write out his lectures which Titus would then
distribute among the students. One important result was that
Titus got to know the doctor very well. He wrote to Titus
later: 'Such readiness to be of help to others made a deep
impression on me, and not only on me but on all who had
contact with you.'

Towards the end of December 1901 Titus suffered a
haemorrhage. He was confined for many weeks to his cell
and forbidden to study, although later in the year his health
improved and he was successful in his final exams. During
the time of ill-health he was allowed visitors, among whom
was Dr Hubertus. Titus wrote in an album presented to Dr
Hubertus on the occasion of his golden jubilee: 'In those
brief moments you told me now this and then that about
your Roman days, about your trials and difficulties, about
your occasionally bold opposition to what you thought to be
wrong, not to make me bitter - that you never did - but to
make me see that something had to be done and could be

done… There is always a turning point. The Lord does not wish things to remain always the same. There are moments in time when people must come forward who are willing and able to change them, not in a spirit of rebellion but from a genuine love of the Order and its continued development.'

Titus was gradually maturing; he came to understand the greatness of his Order, its worldwide nature. But he also saw that there must be differences of opinion and conflicting views, as in any family. He was being prepared for his own apostolate in the Carmelite Order and in the world. In September 1902 Titus left Boxmeer for Zenderen to begin the four year course in theology. After one year at Zenderen and two years at Oss he was ordained a priest on 17th June 1905. A year later he completed his course.

The general view was that he was destined for higher studies in Rome, but his independence of mind had alienated his professor, Dr Eugenius Driessen, Hubertus's brother. He vetoed the move. Titus was deeply disappointed, but made no complaint. The return of Hubertus to Holland, however, led to the breaking down of opposition. Titus made his own position quite clear – he could not accept without question everything he was told, nor could he expect others to do so; speaking to his Provincial, he said: 'You know what an independent mind I have.' His Provincial replied: 'That is precisely why you should go to Rome, so that you can study philosophy better.'

Like many others Titus fell in love with Rome. He stayed at St Albert's College, later to become the Order's International College, where he found himself in contact with Carmelites from all over the world. He studied at the Gregorian University not only philosophy but also 'physics', which included geometry, mathematics, physiology and astronomy. He was not satisfied with this and was allowed to follow a course in sociology too. This proved of major importance since it made him aware of the enormous possibilities open for priests and others to make their mark in bringing Christianity into the centre of national life. His health, however, was not good and, especially in his third and final year, he lost many months of study. At the first attempt he failed the examinations for his doctorate. Nevertheless, he had been appointed as teacher of philosophy at Oss; in October 1909 he returned to Rome, receiving his doctorate of Divinity. He was twenty-eight.

Professor and Journalist

Sent to teach philosophy to the Dutch Carmelite students at Oss, Titus did not limit himself to this work. He was continually asked to undertake a variety of activities, all of which brought into the open his efficiency and his tact. His first venture was in the realm of journalism with the publication of Carmelrozen, a magazine dedicated to the Mother of God and intended to make Carmel better known to the general public. Within a year of publication there were already eleven thousand subscribers. In 1916 he began to think of extending his earlier work on St Teresa of Avila, a project which proved very successful and eventually involved the translation of all her works into Dutch in seven volumes. Titus himself was responsible for the first publication – her Autobiography – in 1918; by 1936 three other parts had appeared and the work was completed after the Second World War.

Titus also became involved in furthering the revival of Frisian culture and language. In 1919 he was asked to become the editor of the local paper which was in danger of collapse and in the same year he was responsible for the setting up of a local library. In addition he had been elected in 1909 to the Carmelite Definitory – the body which advised the Carmelite Provincial – and he remained a member for most of the rest of his life.

During this period Titus was still at his desk at half past one in the morning, even though at 6.30 a.m. he would be offering Mass and in school at 8 a.m. From its beginnings on Mount Carmel at the beginning of the thirteenth century the Carmelite Order has always striven to combine contemplation with the apostolate, although at times this has been difficult. Titus once said: 'Inevitably, in almost all the circumstances of modern life, the active apostolate makes its great demands on Carmel. This activity must be rooted in contemplation, since this is its source and warrant of fruitfulness.'

Apostle for Christ

'The love of Christ urges me on.' These words of the apostle Paul characterise the activity of Titus Brandsma during the years between the First and Second World Wars. Appointed teacher of philosophy at the new Catholic University of Nijmegen in 1923 he not only took the academic side of his work seriously but was keenly interested in the students themselves. The student-friars of those days recalled that his interest in them was 'not something passing, but genuine, personal and all-embracing, it extended beyond our studies. He often joined us and showed an interest in our hobbies.'

He became known as 'ons profke' – our little professor. His was an open door for all and sundry; his housekeeper at times expressed her worry and wanted to stop visitors, but Titus replied: 'But it would be sure to be the one who really needed my help. You'd better let him in.'

His interests ranged far and wide – the establishment of a shrine to St Boniface at Dokkum in Frisia, where the saint had been murdered, and the Stations of the Cross there for which he wrote some meditations while under arrest; the planning of a definitive history of Frisian mysticism; the expansion of University life; the rebuilding of the Carmelite church in Mainz; the opening of a Carmelite house in Nijmegen itself, of which he became the first Prior; the arranging of a series of important lectures on mysticism; the preparation of the first National Marian Congress and pilgrimage in 1932; his appointment as Rector Magnificus of the University of Nijmegen for the academic year 1932–33, which he opened with an address on the Concept of God which aroused enormous interest both in and outside the Order; his researches and lectures on mysticism which led him to France, Italy, Spain, Germany and the United States of America, where he spoke eloquently on Carmelite mysticism; his appointment in 1935 by the Dutch Hierarchy as National Spiritual Adviser to Catholic Journalists; his apostolate for the Reunion of Christendom; and so much more.

Fr Malachy Lynch, remembered in England as the well-beloved Prior of The Friars, Aylesford, had vivid memories of Titus and his tireless industry: 'It was so quietly done, so naturally that one might easily have overlooked it. He was a great example of a priest, fully alive and with a sense of cheerful urgency.' Fr Malachy recalled that his most vivid memory of Titus was of him sitting behind his typewriter puffing happily at a cigar. Titus frequently smoked cigars (cigars in Holland are as commonplace as cigarettes in England) or his pipe; the greater his concentration, the more he smoked.

The Carmelite

'Elijah was above all the great contemplative; but God called him many times from his contemplation to the active life, and his place in the history of Israel is as one of its most untiring labourers. He always returned to the solitude of the life of contemplation. So the Carmelites must be contemplatives who from their active life always return to contemplation as to the higher and better part of their vocation.'

So spoke Titus in his lectures on Carmelite mysticism at the Catholic University of Washington on 16 July 1935. For him, 'The life of Elijah is the shortest summary of the Order's life.'

Titus not only spoke about Carmelite mysticism but lived it. Unfortunately he was extremely reticent about his own personal spiritual life and we only rarely get a glimpse of it. Although he enjoyed travelling – he had a season ticket on the trains – he preferred to be in Carmel. In prayer he gave the impression of being perfectly calm and absorbed in God. On one occasion he said to his audience: 'God who lives in us and in whom we live and move and have our being does not always hide… Sometimes he replaces the image by the reality, the imagination by the conscious experience. In Holland, too, he has done so.' It is not unlikely that he was referring to his own experience.

Whenever possible he would be in choir at 5.30 each morning for meditation. He was determined to live the Carmelite Rule as fully as possible. The Divine Office was a tonic for him, reviving his strength; when entering the chapel he seemed to leave behind all his worldly activities and became absorbed in his worship, so much so that at times his voice resounded too loudly, and this had to be pointed out to him. At one time there was a discussion in the Definitory about exempting the student-friars from the Office; Titus reacted strongly: 'If that is going to be tabled in the Definitory, I shall speak out against it with all available energy. If there is anyone who has grounds for exemption, it is me and I won't dream of it.'

At the same time he was consistently practical and realistic. If the friars could work better in more adequately heated rooms, they must have them – that was no luxury, nor was the provision of periodicals and books. Visitors were welcome and were offered cigars and tea. While he was most zealous in the keeping of the Carmelite Rule, he never allowed this observance to become mere routine, for that could be an obstacle to union with God.

Titus would not have been a true Carmelite if he did not have a tender yet genuine love for the Mother of Carmel. He thought and spoke of Mary with a deep love, recognising that in God's plan of Redemption Jesus and Mary could not be separated. In his book, The Beauty of Carmel, based on his lectures at Washington in 1935, he wrote: 'The mystery of the Incarnation has revealed to us how valuable man is to God, how intimately God wants to be united to man. This wonder draws one's attention to the eternal birth of the Son from the Father as the deepest reason for the mystery of love… The contemplation of this mystery has led to a twofold devotion to Mary, which we had better describe as an imitation, gradually deepening into a close union with her. One should not think of the imitation without thinking of the union nor of the union without the thought of the imitation.'

For this reason he loved to wear the white cloak of Carmel, signifying as it does the maternal protection of Mary. Referring to her title of Theotokos (God-bearer), bestowed on her by the Council of Ephesus, Titus wrote: 'It is our calling to be, after her, Theotokos, God-bearers in the world.' Because of, rather than in spite of, his deep union with God, Titus was also the most human of men, one to whom people flocked in their troubles, for they knew that he would help them. He was a sympathetic listener and those who came to him received both spiritual and material help. 'Our love must be proverbial,' he once preached. 'No one is to surpass us in love.'

Once he went to the help of a girl who had nearly ruined her life; on another occasion he was able to persuade a mentally ill student to become a voluntary patient. Until his arrest he regularly went each Sunday morning to an old people's home to celebrate Mass as they could not afford the usual stipend.

Titus had indeed made his own the words of St Teresa of Avila which he was to have before his eyes in his prison cell: 'Let nothing disturb thee; let nothing dismay thee. All things pass; God never changes. Patience attains all that it strives for. He who has God finds he lacks nothing. God alone suffices.'

Last Days of Freedom

On 10 May 1940 Hitler's armies invaded Holland without warning; within a few days the country was forced to capitulate and slowly but inexorably the German forces began their deliberate attempts to curtail the freedom of the people.

In the course of 1937 Titus's health had begun to give way. One day he told his Prior: 'I am afraid that there is something wrong. I can't keep standing up any more. My knees are failing me.' He looked exhausted, his memory began to fail and he had spells of giddiness. The doctors diagnosed an infection of the spinal marrow. Later that year a serious infection of the urinary tract complicated matters. Titus tried to show himself as cheerful as before and slowly his health over the next two years improved. From now till his death in 1942 many of these symptoms recurred, but in no way did they diminish his apostolic zeal.

After the occupation of Holland, the Nazis directed their attacks against the Jews, the Press and religious schools. From May 1941 no priest or religious was allowed to be head of any educational establishment, while the salaries of those who lived in religious communities was cut by sixty per cent, making it well-nigh impossible for them to carry on their schools. At the request of the Catholic Education Council in Holland Titus travelled up and down the country in defence of Jewish children who were receiving a Catholic education; he strove to make known to the Nazis that 'the Church in carrying out her mission makes no distinction between sex, race or people.'

On 31st December 1941 Titus wrote to his brother Henry, a Franciscan: 'The Lord grant you joy above all. Try to live calmly and be relaxed; have confidence in God, come what may, for he is always with you. Give yourself up quietly to his Providence.'

On that same morning Titus had sat in the study of the Archbishop of Utrecht, Archbishop Jan de Jong; they were discussing the order which had just been issued that the Catholic Press must carry advertisements on behalf of the Nazi Party. Titus was there in his capacity as National Spiritual Adviser to Catholic journalists, a post to which he had been appointed in 1935. The issue was clearly a matter of conscience. Titus had agreed to act on behalf of the Dutch Hierarchy. Archbishop de Jong wrote later: 'I always admired him for his courage and vision… I consider him a martyr.'

The mandate given to Titus was to inform the editors of the Catholic Press that it was impossible for their newspapers to carry Nazi advertisements and remain Catholic publications. To that effect he wrote them letters, intending to deliver them personally in the New Year of 1942. He wrote: 'The Hierarchy acknowledges that as long as editors and directors strive to maintain the specific Catholic character of their paper their striving deserves respect and acknowledgement. But… there is no doubt that the order which was issued a few days ago by the leading elements in the Press makes the carrying out of that order a definite infringement of Catholic principles. This is the order that forces editors to accept advertisements from the National Socialist Party and which explicitly states the refusal on grounds of principle is not tolerated. The leaders are themselves hereby deliberately making an issue out of a principle. Catholic papers cannot comply. The order has not yet been made official. The papers have received the instruction via the telex. It is possible that it will not be made official. So much the better. But if it should happen or if such advertisements as referred to in the telex instruction were placed, the directors and editors must refuse their publication if they value the Catholic character of their newspaper, even though they are threatened with a fine or suspension, or worse, with the liquidation of the paper concerned. We have reached the limit. I trust that in this matter the Catholic newspapers will maintain the Catholic position.'

The next few days were crucial. Titus travelled throughout Holland delivering his message and discussing its implications with editors and members of the Hierarchy. But someone betrayed him and disclosed his mission to the German authorities. On 7th January 1942 the Nazi in charge of Press affairs, Willy Janke, dictated a memorandum to the Generalkommissar, Herr Schmidt, requesting the immediate arrest of Fr Brandsma; at the same time he was listed as a candidate for a concentration camp.

Unaware of the impending threat, Titus continued his travels, meeting with the Archbishop on Saturday 10th January. A few yards from the Archbishop's House the leaders of the Nazi Party were deciding not to place advertisements in the Catholic papers: but it was too late for their decision to affect Fr Brandsma's fall.

Titus himself became aware of his danger. 'The Germans are after me, they say that I am committing sabotage. They don't understand at all. But I am going to carry on. Let them arrest me.'

He carried on his work as usual. He had asked the Catholic editors to remain firm; he could not himself suddenly disappear. When people mentioned the danger he was in, Titus remarked: 'Now I am going to get what has seldom been my lot, and what I have always wanted: a cell of my own. Now at last I shall be a real Carmelite.'

Strangers had already been asking for him at the Carmelite Priory in Nijmegen, but he had been away. On Monday 19th January, Titus celebrated Mass in Amsterdam for the last time in his life in the church dedicated to St Boniface. After a visit to the Department of Education at the Hague, Titus returned to Nijmegen where he delivered his first lecture after the Christmas holidays. That evening, at about six o'clock, he was arrested by Sicherheitspolizei – the secret police – and spent the night in a cell at Arnhem. The following day he was taken to the prison in Scheveningen near the Hague.

A 'hotel' in Scheveningen

Titus was to spend the next seven weeks in this prison, nicknamed 'the hotel' by the inmates. On 18th February his first letter arrived at the priory in Nijmegen and was soon circulated among his relatives and colleagues. They read: 'I am already at home here. I pray, I read, I write, the days are too short. I am very calm, happy and contented.'

His cell was bleak. Through the window above the door he could see only the sky, although 'now and again a seagull passes.' He was allowed to smoke and was given back his watch even though to set it he had to guess the hour.

He still had his breviary: this he opened and placed above his bed open at the page showing the Madonna of Carmel: 'At my table I have only to look a little to the right and I have her image before me. When I am in bed, my eye catches at once the star-bearing Madonna, the hope of all Carmelites.' On his desk he placed a picture of Christ crucified and wrote out the famous words of St Teresa: 'Let nothing disturb thee… ' and, 'God so near and far, God is always there.' He missed his Mass and Holy Communion but knew that God was always with him.

The whole attitude and happiness of Titus is well expressed in a poem he wrote in Scheveningen and which has become well-known:

Dear Lord, when looking up to Thee,
I see Thy loving eyes on me;
Love overflows my humble heart,
Knowing what faithful friend Thou art.

A cup of sorrow I foresee,
Which I accept for love of Thee.
The painful way I wish to go
The only way to God I know.

My soul is full of peace and light;
Although in pain this light shines bright.
For here thou keepest to Thy breast
My longing heart, to find there rest.

Leave me here freely alone,
In cell where never sunlight shone;
Should no one ever speak to me,
This golden silence makes me free!

For though alone, I have no fear;
Never wert Thou, O Lord, so near.
Sweet Jesus, please, abide with me;
My deepest peace I find in Thee.

(Translated by Albert Groeneveld)

Titus had here in Scheveningen found his true vocation;
here in his solitary cell he made his last retreat; for the last
time he returned to the joys of contemplation from the mul-

tifarious activities of his previous life. 'Beata solitudo (Bless solitude)... I am completely at home in this little cell. I haven't been bored once. On the contrary, I am alone, yes, but never has the good Lord been so near to me. I could shout for joy that he has allowed himself to be found by me, without me meeting people or people meeting me. He is now my sole refuge and I feel safe and happy. I am willing to remain here always, if he will allow me. Rarely have I been so happy and contented.'

This happiness radiated from his face, as is testified by many who came in contact with him during this period.

Apart from his breviary Titus was allowed two other books, Jesus by Cyriel Vershaeve and a life of St Teresa of Avila by Kwakman. He was himself working on a biography of Teresa which was later published.

On the evening of 21st January Hardegan, the head of the secret police department at the Hague dealing with the Churches, told Titus that he was being held 'for clarification.' Many were the times that Titus himself tells us that Hardegan was always courteous; he used his own intelligence and asked his own questions, not those prepared by others. Titus was questioned about his attitude and his 'sabotage', as Hardegan described it. At the end of one interview, Titus stated quite clearly: 'When measures are taken which are irreconcilable with Catholic teaching, the Church is obliged to refute them. I am told that I am under arrest until this affair is cleared up. But one thing I must make clear: the attitude of the Dutch Hierarchy is my own.'

He even courageously admitted to his questioner that he would act no differently if a similar situation were to arise again. In addition to these interrogations, Titus was given paper and pen and told to provide a written reply to the question, 'Why does the Dutch nation, especially its Catholic population, oppose the N.S.B. (the Dutch Nazi Party).'

He answered at length and with his usual honesty: 'The suppression of the religious ecclesiastical influence is not only an offence to God in relation to his creatures, but a violation of the glorious traditions of the Dutch people. Herein lies the heart of the matter.' He ended his formal reply: 'God bless the Netherlands. God bless Germany. God grant both nations, so akin to each other in many ways to come together in peace and unity, and to stand next to one another in recognition of God and his honour.' Hardegan was under no illusions about Titus: he called him 'a very dangerous little man.'

Number 58 in the hell of Amersfoot

On 12th March 1942 several large police cars with canvas covers drove out of the prison gate of Scheveningen; they held a hundred prisoners; among them was Fr Brandsma. That evening the cars arrived at the gates of the concentration camp at Amersfoot near Utrecht.

After being stripped naked and kept standing in the bitter cold for hours, Titus and the other prisoners were finally issued with the old Dutch soldier's uniform with the matching cap and a pair of wooden shoes. His head was completely shaven and on his uniform was a red triangle to classify him as a political prisoner. Titus was now just one of a crowd – No. 58. There was no more questioning. For the next six weeks Titus endured all the sufferings and humiliations of a concentration camp – the cramped conditions, freezing cold, work from eight in the morning till six at night, the cruelty of the guards, physical exhaustion, dysentery, starvation and malnutrition.

It was not long before everyone knew who he was. He was to be seen in the company of the greatest variety of prisoners and had a kindly smile and a word for all. As one of the prisoners later recalled, 'He gave us a supernatural insight into our imprisonment.'

Many came to him for courage and strength; he blessed them all, shaking hands with them and making the sign of the cross on their hand with his thumb, for any outward mark of religion was strictly forbidden.

A recent order meant that religious subjects could no longer be discussed in the camp. But on Good Friday, 3rd April, Titus found a way of meditating with the prisoners on the Passion of Jesus. He started his talk with a piece of genuine history – the place of the fourteenth century writer and preacher Geert Groote in Dutch literature. In front of him were his hundred or so guests – professors, doctors, Protestant ministers, priests, lawyers and journalists, together with many of a less academic background – all dressed in the shabby soldiers' uniform, suffering and half-starved. His lecture continued to develop the history of mysticism until he was led into a meditation on the 'Passion of Jesus, the first object of our contemplation.' As he gazed on his audience, he must have been struck by the parallel between their lives and the life of Christ in the last days of his earthly pilgrimage.

It was a meditation which made an indelible impression on all who listened, on those who 'were making up in their bodies what was lacking in the sufferings of Christ for his Body, the Church.' As one of them recalled, 'Quietly we went back to our places. Struck by God's Spirit, no one said a word.'

Thanks to the prisoners who escaped death, we have abundant testimonies of those days in Amersfoot. One witness remembered Titus especially: 'He towered above them. He made me feel that I had met a saint.' At the same time the witness stresses that Titus was not disinterested in his fate nor insensitive. 'He (Titus) tried not to show it, but at times he was deeply saddened, not because of self-pity, but because of the knowledge, constantly before him, that men could do such things to one another. He never allowed his mental suffering to diminish his humour. He merely became quieter, more compassionate. Even for the bad element amongst the prisoners he always had kind and gentle words.'

These difficult hours were noted by another priest-prisoner: 'Only in very intimate conversations did his sadness reveal itself, and always in complete surrender to God.'

Towards Dachau

On 6th May the telephone rang in the Prior's room at Nijmegen. He was astounded to hear the voice of Fr Brandsma. Titus was back in the prison in Scheveningen where he had arrived on 28th April, once again wearing his black clerical suit. Several times he was taken to the headquarters of the secret police and questioned by Hardegan, who asked him once again to reply in writing to the familiar question concerning the opposition of the Dutch Catholic Church to the Nazi Party. Titus had been allowed to speak to the Prior only to inform him that he was on his way to Dachau, where he would remain till the end of the war.

At the prison he shared a cell with two young prisoners, both of whom believed in God. They talked to each other easily and happily; they joined together in prayer and on the Feast of the Ascension Titus spoke to them about the gifts of the Holy Spirit. One of them later remembered: 'Those were great moments in our lives.'

Titus's second stay at Scheveningen lasted less than a month. On Saturday 16th May, the feast of St Simon Stock, for whom Titus had such a great devotion as the saint to whom Mary offered her special protection in the form of the Carmelite scapular, he crossed the Dutch-German border and found himself at the transit camp of Kleve.

Conditions here were comparatively good; the food was well-cooked though lacking in quantity. Titus admitted on one occasion that he was ravenously hungry, yet he still gave some of his food away to the Italian who shared his cell.

The curate in Kleve, Ludwig Deimel, was also prison chaplain. Once again Titus had the happiness of receiving Holy Communion, although there was no way in which he could celebrate Mass. It was also through the chaplain that Fr Brandsma made an appeal to be released and placed in some monastery under house arrest; he based his plea on his continued ill-health, which gave him periods of dizziness and loss of memory and left him deathly tired all day long. Since this was addressed to the German authorities, it was a case of special pleading; those who knew him in Kleve stated that he was always in possession of his spiritual faculties and that his appearance was 'very fine and spiritualised.'

Outside the prison many others were making efforts to get him released, but all to no avail.

Titus was essentially a realistic man; he did not desire martyrdom or extraordinary suffering nor, on the other hand, did he expect ecstasies. He did his best to remain alive as long as it was possible to do so and as long as he could be of service to others. On the other hand, when

God's way became clear to him, he accepted it gladly and willingly. During his first stay at Scheveningen he had expressed his point of view in this way: 'I suffer with joy what has to be suffered for sticking to one's principles. My vocation to the Church and to the priesthood has given me so much that is wonderful that I am equally pleased to take up something that is unpleasant. So far it is not so bad. And although I don't know what is to happen, I put myself entirely in God's hands. Who shall separate me from the love of God?'

Dachau

On Saturday 13th June, the hour of departure from Kleve arrived. Fr Brandsma was chained and with his companions put on the transport train for the concentration camp a few miles outside Dachau in Bavaria. The journey itself took six days; it is very difficult to reconstruct what happened. It seems that the cell-cars travelled through Cologne, which had just undergone a heavy bombardment, then Frankfurt, Mainz, and Nuremburg. At Nuremburg the prisoners were housed in the Turnhalle, a vast gymnasium. Someone later described it as a 'great receptacle of European misery.' On the day after they arrived there, they were given only two slices of bread and some coffee; a single fountain stood in a corner from which hundreds of men had to drink. Barrels stood at strategic points to serve as lavatories; the stench became overpowering during the two or three days they were kept there. On 19th June their train steamed into Dachau.

The prisoners were handcuffed again, stripped and made to undergo the humiliating procedure of 'vermin control'. Then, dressed in blue-grey trousers and jackets, wooden sandals and ridiculous looking caps, they were instructed in the ways of saluting, marching, and making their beds. At last, Titus, now No. 30492, was led to Block 28, where the Polish priests were imprisoned.

Our knowledge of the events leading to the death of Fr Brandsma comes from fellow-prisoners who miraculously survived Dachau. The day began at 4 a.m. with a siren call. The quicker he got dressed, the more time Titus had for making his bed in the expected manner – he was never very good at this. Then to the washroom, where he ate what little food had been saved from the previous evening, and to the roll-call ground for the counting. This was an opportunity for a short whispered greeting and private prayer. Five o'clock came and off the prisoners went to join the work squad. Titus and a hundred others were marched to the 'Liebhof' garden, accompanied by the SS men and dogs. Here in the garden they had to dig the heavy soil and plant medicinal herbs. They wore wooden shoes and before long Titus's feet showed a number of big ulcerating wounds. They worked ceaselessly from 5.30 a.m. to 11.30 a.m. on practically empty stomachs, without rest or water. Then they were marched back to the camp for a half-hour's break to eat the miserable soup with a few vegetables. After that brief respite they were marched back to the fields where they worked till seven o'clock in the evening. On return, they again suffered the roll-call, which could last for an hour, after which they collected their rations. These had to suffice for the following morning – three and a half ounces of bread with a little butter and a couple of potatoes. For the priests – 'those hated ministers of God' – the day was still not ended, for very often they were forced to do an extra half-hour's exercise of marching and press-ups. Finally, around nine o'clock, they were able to retire.

Many prisoners died in the 'Liebhof', nicknamed by the prisoners the 'Friedhof' (cemetery). Frequently, Titus had to be helped back to the camp. Walter Thiel, the SS man who reigned supreme, was a brute of a man who cruelly ill-treated Titus and the others. Once he was seen to beat Titus in the face with his bowl, opening a wound which bled freely on Titus's emaciated face.

Titus was unable to face the physical conditions of the camp and he also seemed to lack the knack of getting out of difficult situations. He became the butt and target of the guards. Once he forgot his glasses and crept inside the block to retrieve them. Thiel discovered him and gave him a terrific blow which threw Titus to the ground where he was again struck over and over again. At last he was able to get up, helped by his Carmelite colleague, Brother Raphael. But Raphael could not always be close.

Despite this cruelty Fr Brandsma remained peaceful in his close union with his crucified Lord. A Polish priest recalls: 'Fr Brandsma was then in pretty bad shape, physically emaciated and weak, but he communicated a great tranquillity of spirit.'

In January 1941, before Titus arrived, the authorities had allowed a small chapel to be built in the block occupied by German priests, and Mass was offered daily. This must have been a great consolation to the other prisoners though they were not permitted to attend. However, a secret system of distributing the consecrated hosts existed. We know that once or twice at the evening meal a Capuchin friar was able to pass the host, hidden between potatoes, to Titus. On one occasion when Titus was carrying the Blessed Sacrament concealed in his spectacle case, Thiel suddenly turned on him, beat and kicked him as if he had gone mad. With his spectacle case tucked under his arm, Titus was able to crawl back to his bunk in Block 28 assisted by Brother Raphael. He waited till Thiel was out of the way, then smiling said: 'I knew whom I had with me.' He suggested that together they should say the Adore te, and quietly blessed his Carmelite colleague.

By 16th July, the Feast of Our Lady of Mount Carmel, it was clear that Titus was completely exhausted. Nothing, however, would stop him from praying for the guards and from trying to bring them back to God and their humanity. 'Who knows? Perhaps something will stick,' he said.

He encouraged his fellow-prisoners: 'We are here in a dark tunnel. We have to pass through it. Somewhere at the end shines the eternal light.' He spoke as much for the guards in their spiritual darkness as for the prisoners.

One morning, Titus stood outside his Block in the drizzling rain with some companions. Seeking a place of shelter, they were beaten up by the guards . Then, we are told, 'the Dutch Carmelite friar (Brother Raphael) went with Titus Brandsma to the prison hospital.'

Titus said good bye and entered the 'hospital'. It was a hospital in name only; prisoners were the subject of biochemical experiments and deliberate infection with malaria. No prisoner would go there except in the last extremity.

Titus remained here for only a few days. He lay on a straw mattress alone and with the minimum of care. He was disgracefully humiliated by the doctors. While they used his body for their own ends, Titus simply said aloud: 'Not my will, but thine be done.'

We know the end through the testimony of the nurse who was with him and whose identity has to remain a secret although her name is known in Rome. Titus discovered that she was a Dutch Catholic and asked her how she had ended up in Dachau. 'I shall pray for you a lot,' he told her. He gave her his rosary, at which she protested: 'I can no longer pray.' Titus exclaimed: 'Well, if you can't say the first part, surely you can still say, "Pray for us sinners."' The other patients constantly surrounded him and he strove to encourage them and to direct their attention to God. Twice he was able to receive Holy Communion.

On 24th July Titus became unconscious. On Sunday 26th July at 1.50 p.m. the nurse gave him the fatal injection and he died at 2 o'clock. Three days later his body was cremated in the camp crematorium.

Beatification

On 3rd November 1985, in St Peter's Basilica, Rome, Pope John Paul II beatified Titus Brandsma. He said of him "In the midst of the onslaughts of hatred, he was able to love – everybody, including his tormentors: 'They too are children of the good God', he said, 'and who knows whether something remains in them…'. Of course, such heroism is not something that can be improvised. Fr Titus spent his whole life bringing it to maturity, from the earliest experience of infancy, living in a deeply Christian family in his beloved Friesland. From the words and example of his parents, from the teaching he heard in the parish Church, from the charitable activities which he experienced in the parish community, he learnt to know and to practise Christ's fundamental commandment of love for everyone, not excluding one's very enemies".